TWO DIFFERENT BOOTS

Two Different Boots

Stepping Out of My Mother's Shadow and Learning to Love the Woman I See

MICHELLE L. SMITH

Two Different Boots, LLC

CONTENTS

~ 1 ~
Two Different Boots: The First Step
1

~ 2 ~
Lesson 1: Do As I Say, Not As I Do
30

~ 3 ~
Lesson 2: My Past Does Not Define Me
37

~ 4 ~
Lesson 3: I Am Not, Nor Will I EVER Be, My Mother
41

~ 5 ~
Lesson 4: Just Because She Gave Birth To Me, I'm Not Obligated To Spend Time With Her
47

~ 6 ~
Lesson 5: This Totally Sucks For My Kids
53

~ 7 ~

Lesson 6: Being A Mom Is Hard Work And There's No Rule Book

57

~ 8 ~

Lesson 7: I Have to Find My Own Closure

63

~ 9 ~

Lesson 8: It's Okay For Me To Forgive

68

~ 10 ~

Lesson 9: Life Must Go On…I Choose To Learn From It

73

~ 11 ~

Lesson 10: I Am Not Alone

77

~ 12 ~

Life Beyond the Lessons

81

~ 13 ~

Conclusion

84

~ 14 ~

Epilogue

86

~ 15 ~
Acknowledgments
90

~ 16 ~
About The Author
93

Copyright © 2021 by Michelle L. Smith
Cover Design: Ryder T. Smith

All rights reserved. No part of this book may be reproduced in any manner whatsoever without written permission except in the case of brief quotations embodied in critical articles and reviews.

~ 1 ~

TWO DIFFERENT BOOTS: THE FIRST STEP

Life.

We have to take it one step at a time.

My journey is unique to me, just like yours is unique to you.

Every step along the way shaped me into who I am today, even the ones where my foot didn't land gracefully.

This is my story.

I'm the middle child of three siblings. I have two brothers, one just over a year older than me and the other five years younger.

Mom came from a family of six. Her parents ran a bar when she was young, which shaped her life (and her siblings' lives) in ways that I'm sure I don't truly understand. She was 5'4 and dark-haired, and beautiful in her prime. I like to think I look a bit like she did "back in the day."

She was a passive person, didn't like conflict much, and tried to avoid it as much as possible. Definitely more of a lover than a fighter.

Dad was a hardworking man, a welder by trade. He was musical and played the guitar. Stood 6 feet tall, dark-haired, and typically sported a beard. He drank a lot, Jack Daniels being his favorite poison. He had a very kind heart, but when he got angry you knew it.

He lost his mom when he was just 11 years old. He had two siblings, but they were quite a bit older and off on their own or in college when their mom passed. So Dad grew up mostly living alone with his father, who was a military man. And then, when his father remarried, had a stepmom who I knew as my grandmother when we were growing up.

Dad passed away 11 years ago, at just 56 years old. His heavy drinking and lack of self-care caught up to him and caused a heart attack. It was tragic and heartbreaking when he passed, but that's a story for a different book.

The relationship I had with my father shaped my life, but not nearly as much as the one I didn't have with my mother.

My mom and dad divorced when I was two years old. Dad moved back to his hometown in Illinois and my older brother and I stayed with Mom in Wisconsin.

Mom remarried shortly after that. Our stepfather was smaller in build than my dad, but tall and dark-haired as well. He was an auto mechanic by trade and, ironically, also played the guitar.

He loved us like we were his own children.

But he also came with his unique life experiences from growing up in a very strict home and that shaped his life and his relationship with my mom.

He and my mom had a child together when I was 5 years old. That's when I became the middle child, sandwiched between two brothers. Brothers who tormented me mercilessly when we were young - but I couldn't imagine life without today.

We were very poor growing up, living on what often felt like little to nothing. Mom didn't work when we were young, and an auto mechanic's salary could only go so far for a family of five. My stepdad worked hard, but it was a struggle.

We ate a lot of soup from a can and meals made with chicken. We were on and off state assistance as I was growing up.

We moved a lot, which was hard for me.

I went to kindergarten at one grade school, and then transferred to a different one when we moved to the next town over. In middle school, I went the first month or so of 7th grade to one school, then switched to another.

This made it difficult to make a strong circle of friends.

Kids are ruthless at that age and they form cliques. And I wasn't the most outgoing person as a child.

I was quiet and introspective, typically carrying a book or a notepad with me everywhere we went so I could read or write. I loved school. But I didn't fit in very well.

I had to wear eyeglasses, and the only ones we could afford were the options covered by Medicaid. Big, brown, ugly plastic frames. They covered my eyes and half my cheeks. I would often get teased that it looked like I had TV sets on my face.

HIgh school was the worst. I had to switch schools my Junior year (to the rival high school no less) and finish my last two years of high school with kids I didn't know and hadn't grown up with.

I didn't feel like I really belonged anywhere or that I had anyone in life to rely on.

The one good thing that came out of those moves was meeting my best friend when I changed schools in 7th grade. She became my rock through some of the most tumultuous times of my life as I navigated being a teenager without a mom to guide me.

Mom was never a very strong person emotionally. She always seemed to be anxious, trying to please everyone and keep the peace. She smoked two to three packs of cigarettes a day, which just made me sick to my stomach and embarrassed by the way I smelled because of it.

It was more normal back then in the 80's but it still made me self-conscious. The smell of cigarettes to this day makes me nauseous.

We only saw Dad every other weekend and he often canceled because he was "sick," which I realized as I got older was code for hungover. I still remember that awful disappointed feeling I would get when I had my bag all packed and we'd hear the phone ring and then Mom would tell us he wasn't coming.

We had bad examples all around us on all sides of our families, people involved in drinking and drugs and making bad choices.

Reading and writing was my solace. I could escape to a whole different world and not see all of the things around me that just made me feel lonely and scared.

I was jealous of my friends with "normal" households. Those with parents who had never been divorced, who had fancy houses and nicer clothes than me.

Because I felt so unstable and ashamed of my home life, I tried to find things that I could hold on to, that were tangible and concrete. I focused on what I could control, which was school, and then work as I got older. I buried myself in my studies, got excellent grades, and found validation in being the smart, responsible one.

I realize now that this was my way to get the attention I so desperately wanted back then. And that need for attention impacted me later on in life too.

When I was very little, mom was there for us. She seemed to be able to handle the younger years when we could sit on her lap and give hugs. We always had hugs goodnight and always an "I Love You" before bed. I have learned that from her and I'm grateful for that as she did teach me how to be tender and loving.

But as we got older and more self-sufficient, probably around school age, she started to disengage with us emotionally. We didn't need the hugs and kisses as much anymore. We needed guidance and support as we grew into our formative years.

Mom wasn't emotionally equipped for that.

You see, my Mom has bipolar depression, although I didn't know that as a young child. She wasn't officially diagnosed with it until well after I was grown. Even if she had been, I doubt that I would have understood it or what it meant for her.

In her manic times, she was a drinker and a partier, and in her depressive times, I watched her withdraw into herself over and over, spending hours upon hours in bed, losing all desire to do anything.

I watched her attempt suicide for the first time when I was 12 years old. She swallowed a bunch of pills at my aunt's house. I remember vividly seeing her walking up to the house from the backyard, my aunt with her arm around her. I don't remember any other details from that day though. I'm pretty sure I've repressed those memories. I know they took her to the hospital, but can't even recall who I stayed with or when she came home.

It was horrible and so scary to see those things. I had no idea why it was happening, what part I played in it, or what I could do to help. And I was ashamed and felt so embarrassed to not have a "normal" mom.

I think that was about the time I started to feel the resentment that I carried with me for so many years. I just couldn't understand why I didn't deserve to have a mom who was there for me. Why my mom thought about herself more than she did her kids.

She wasn't emotionally available to teach me how to take care of things when I got my first period. She wasn't there when I broke up with my first boyfriend and needed her to tell me it would all be okay. She wasn't there time and time again. I eventually just stopped thinking she ever would be and didn't bother talking to her about any of it.

My relationship with my stepfather was good, but I couldn't talk to him about the things I needed to talk to my mom about. He was always working. He came from a family where hard work and schooling were most important, so I did as well as I could in school to get his attention and make him proud of me.

My biological father and I had a good relationship, when I did see him, which was maybe once or twice a month depending on whether he showed up on weekends. I couldn't see how he could help my situation. He had his own demons.

I didn't feel like I could talk about any of this with my extended family, either. Mom came from a long family history of poor health and challenges with mental illness. Whenever we would talk about her, it just felt like they would make excuses and minimize her behavior.

I always felt that they took her side. *Your mom is just depressed, she's doing the best she can.* I would hear that often. I would think, "but what about me, what about my brothers? We matter too! We deserve to have a mother!"

I was scared, angry, and felt very, very alone.

After she divorced my stepdad, it got even worse. They had been married for 10 years or so, with lots of challenges that even now I don't fully understand. All I knew is that my family was breaking up (again).

My little brother moved several hours away with his dad and I lost touch with him for a few years. Mom retreated further into her own world, but took my older brother and me on the ride with her.

I was barely a teenager at the time and my mom, my brother and I lived in a tiny, rundown upstairs apartment. Mom was never there.

She worked two part-time jobs and when she wasn't working, she'd go out with her friends and drink and bring home strange men. I'd lock my bedroom door and hide under the covers, wishing for them to leave, freezing every time I heard footsteps outside of my room.

From my vantage point, she was too busy running around, selfishly living her own life, and pretty much ignoring her kids to be a mom to us. She was choosing herself over us.

My brother and I had lots of freedom, more than teenagers should have. And we took advantage of it, spending time with questionable people, dabbling in underage drinking, and having parties when Mom wasn't home.

My brother protected me though, he made sure that I was always safe. But there were plenty of opportunities for really bad things to happen. I'm grateful to this day that the choices I made back then didn't impact my future in an extremely negative way.

Somehow through it all, the desire to make my life better than what I saw all around me was very strong. I knew how important it was for me to graduate high school, go to college, and have a career of my own. So I never missed school, and I participated in extracurricular activities, and I did my best to make my teachers (and any other adult I encountered) proud.

The older I got though, and the more she wasn't home, the more I resented my mom. She was supposed to be the mother, the responsible one, not us! My brother and I did much of the food shopping, the cleaning, and got ourselves off to school. Yes, we were teenagers by then and capable of doing lots of things on our own, but it was almost like she didn't exist. She had her boyfriends and her drinking buddies.

We were basically on our own.

We were still very poor and had state assistance to buy food. Back then, state assistance meant food stamp coupons, not the credit cards people get today. And when you shopped with them, it was obvious to the people in line with you that you were "poor."

I still remember how embarrassed I felt pulling out those coupons at the grocery store, always checking to see if anyone I knew was in line before we checked out.

If there were people there that we knew, my brother and I would often wait to check out until our friends had left the store, wandering the aisles for just a few more minutes so they didn't see us.

I resented her for putting us through that. I lost respect for her for allowing her children to shoulder that burden.

Now that I'm older, I'm sure she was embarrassed too on some level. But as a child, even a teenage one, I didn't have that perspective. I just wanted life to be normal, to have my mom be able to afford groceries like everyone else, to have her think about us and how this made us feel.

Now that I'm older, I think about the "normal" life I wished I would have had. As a child, I had a vision, probably one that I got from TV, of a typical, loving family where everyone got along, who always had nice family dinners together, where no one did anything embarrassing and everyone around them loved them. I wanted other people to look at our family and be inspired by how great we were.

Idealistic? Yes.
Achievable? Maybe not.

But not even remotely close to what life felt like for me back then.

I remember one pivotal moment in my life that pretty much solidified it for me. I was fifteen. I had won tickets to a concert at Alpine Valley, an outdoor music theatre about 45 minutes from home. I had a friend who had a driver's license and could take me; we just needed a vehicle.

Mom promised that we could use her car. The morning of the concert, she disappeared and didn't come home for three days. I had no idea where she was or when she was coming home.

This was before cell phones, so all I could do was sit at home and wonder, and wait and feel angry and resentful and sad and neglected.

For THREE days!

It was a heart-wrenching experience.

To this day, when I think about it, the anger is there, sweeping through me like a tidal wave.

I don't remember ever getting a good answer from her on why she disappeared, nor a true apology, either. Which just makes it worse.

Even now, hearing songs by George Thorogood brings back those ugly feelings. It's one of my triggers.

During those three days when all I could do was wait and wonder where she was, I swore to myself that I would be nothing like her. That when I became a mom my kids would have a stable home and a mother who was always there for them. Always.

That was and still is a powerful, defining moment in my life.

When I was sixteen, Mom got married for the third time, and I was forced to move with her to the next town over. My older brother went to live with my dad in Illinois.

I had to start a new high school in my Junior year. To make matters worse, my new school was the rival school of the one I had been attending. I was leaving my friends behind to become the enemy.

I knew no one there, everyone had their cliques and their friendships that had been established since childhood.

Walking into that new school on the first day felt like walking into a prison.

This didn't help with the level of resentment I felt toward my mother. It was very hard for me to understand why she would force me to change schools at such a pivotal time in my life.

Again, I felt alone and very, very lonely. All I really wanted was for my mom to hold me and tell me it was all going to be okay. But she never did.

I focused again on my schoolwork, made a few friends in choir, the drama club, and the Academic Decathlon. I worked hard and graduated third in my high school class of 350+ students.

I moved out of my mom's house right after high school into the dorms at the local college about 10 miles away. I was so grateful to be out, and I barely looked back, only staying there on Christmas and summer breaks. After the dorm requirements were over, I moved into an apartment off-campus where I could live year-round.

Mom's new husband had a good job, at least for the first few years I was in college. Just enough to make our household income too high for me to qualify for grants for school. There was no financial help there for me at all.

There was a small trust fund on my Dad's side of the family that I was able to leverage, but the rest of my schooling was fully my responsibility.

I was determined to make it work, though. I knew college was my way out of the life I had been living. My doorway to a better future.

Fortunately, working hard in high school helped a lot. I applied for and received several scholarships to help pay for college.

I took out loans and worked my way through college to pay for the rest of my tuition and book fees, often working 30+ hours per week with a full class load.

I was proving to the world that I could do this, in spite of the fact that my mom wasn't there to support me.

Ultimately, Mom's third marriage didn't work out either.

I was in college working at a local law office part-time when she and her husband made the decision.

They lived in a rundown trailer park at the time. Going to visit them was awful, as they both smoked multiple packs of cigarettes a day. The trailer smelled so much like smoke that I could hardly bear it. The walls and curtains were yellow from all of the tar and smoke residue.

I tried to avoid going to see her, always having an excuse. College was a good one. Between school and work, I could always keep myself busy.

When they decided to divorce, she didn't have the money to pay an attorney. She asked me to help her write up and file her divorce papers. I did because I felt sorry for her.

I was grown enough at that time to realize the role reversal in that situation. I recognized it for what it was, and realized that this had been part of what I had been feeling through much of my formative years.

I was the parent, and she was the child.

A few years after graduating college, I got married and started a family of my own.

That's when I started building the walls. I was creating my own life, and showing the world what I thought they should see to be proud of me, to respect me, to maybe even be inspired by me.

And the walls blocked out the pain and loneliness that I felt, they covered the holes in my heart.

I was excellent at my job, making a decent salary and working for a company with a lot of growth opportunities for me. I wanted to make sure I had a solid financial foundation before having children, so I worked hard to establish myself in my career before becoming a mom.

I became very close with my brothers around this time as well and reconnected with my younger brother when he was able to move back closer to home.

My husband and I started spending more time with the few cousins and aunts who actually had their lives together. My mom's older sister became like a second mother to me.

I grew a bit closer with my dad too in these years. We shared a special trip to Washington State for my cousin's wedding, which was when he and I both fell in love with Mt. Rainier. I've tried to go there every year since Dad passed away to celebrate his birthday.

I was finding ways to build a community around me that helped to fill the void I felt. And with the walls up, I didn't have to let people see how it had felt growing up. I thought I could just put it all behind me.

I thought I was in a good place.

When I was 28 years old, I had my first child. And that's when I started to notice a change again in how I felt about life. Even though I loved my career and felt very secure in my abilities at work, I was unsettled and unhappy and unsure of myself in the other (more important) areas of my life.

There was a part of me that knew from the beginning of my marriage (maybe even before we actually got married) that I hadn't chosen the right partner. There had been signs even back when we were dating, but I don't think I was confident enough in myself to let them come to the surface.

Or maybe I just had no idea what I was really looking for back then.

We were two very different people, who had different ideas of what parenting is, and different ambitions in life. I underestimated how much things would change when we had children.

I wish now that I had known the right questions to ask to build our relationship in a deeper way before we got married.

But I didn't. In your early 20's you just don't know what you need to know.

I didn't know myself back then, or what I really wanted from life. And I had very few examples of strong partnerships to model mine after.

At 32, we had our second child. I was working 50+ hours a week at a company an hour from home, and playing a full-time role as mother, wife, and homemaker. It was an incredibly stressful time.

And I knew in my heart of hearts that my marriage was failing.

For five years, I felt like I wasn't succeeding in any area of it. I was only one person and there just wasn't enough of me to go around.

The pressure was excruciating. And I couldn't show people that I was struggling. I just kept throwing the pain and fear and frustration over those walls and covering it up.

I had come so far, I had worked so hard to make something of my life. I couldn't let people see that I was struggling. I couldn't admit that I felt like a failure so much of the time.

It finally hit a breaking point for me. When I was 37-years-old, my husband and I decided it was time to divorce.

It was the hardest decision of my life. I had sworn that I wouldn't be like my mother, and here I was, going down the same path she did!

I vowed that my boys wouldn't go through what I went through, that they would see their father and I have a healthy, positive relationship. And that they would always feel loved and supported.

Even though it was one of the most difficult things I've ever gone through, I truly believe we've both been better off since then.

We have a stronger relationship now than we did while we were married and we co-parent together to help our boys navigate the world. He got remarried this year, and my boyfriend and I celebrated with them at their wedding. I toasted the bride and groom and hugged my boys and welcomed their new stepmom officially into our family.

My divorce was the turning point for me. It was the beginning of my journey to break down the walls I had built and to find a way to become truly, completely, authentically me.

The weekend I moved out of our family home and into my apartment, I sat on the couch in my new living room and wept.

I wept for the life I thought I should have had.
I wept for the woman who didn't feel complete.
I wept for my boys and the impact I hoped this wouldn't have on them.

And then I wiped the tears away and I knew. It was time for me to move forward.

I had to figure this out, to find a way to feel settled and balanced and learn to truly love myself.

Not the me on the outside, who held it all together at work, and at home. Not the me who was uber-organized and responsive and the mom who was active in the PTO.

But the me that existed under all of that. The me as an independent woman, a unique, whole person.

I was resolved to not subject my boys to the same fate that I had. The desire for them to never feel about me the way I do about my mom was so strong I could almost taste it. That was a powerful motivator for me.

The boys' father and I shared custody and we lived just a mile or so away from each other, which helped make transitions easier for them.

It also gave me time to process and find out who I was on my own, in every sense of the word.

I started to read more self-development books, especially by authors like Brene Brown (*The Power of Vulnerability* and *Rising Strong*) and John C. Maxwell (*The Difference Maker*).

I went to therapy.

I spent time just sitting and reflecting on my life.

I journaled a lot, just letting all the feelings out.

When I didn't have the boys, I spent time with friends, having fun, singing karaoke, drinking too much. Then going on dates to try to figure out what the right partner for me might look like.

I let myself learn who I was, even the parts of me that didn't always do the right thing. I made plenty of mistakes, I kissed some frogs along the way, and I found out what my non-negotiables were.

When I was able to truly see the different sides of myself, it started to become more clear.

I excelled at my job and other structured tasks in life. I was confident and secure and respected at the office. I could run my household like a boss, never missing appointments, bills always on time, paperwork in order.

But when it came to parenting my boys or being in a relationship, man did I struggle! I never felt like I was ever getting it right!

All signs started pointing back to the resentment and anger I harbored toward my mother. To my fear of turning out like her.

And even more specifically, toward her lack of emotional support and guidance in my life and how that shaped me, and how I felt about myself, as a mom and a woman.

I had to take a deep dive into that. I had to look at it from all angles and find ways to learn from my childhood and how it felt to not have a mom who was able to support me the way I needed.

I had to try to understand my mother and what this experience with her had taught me. I had to break down the walls.

When I was young, I had no idea what bipolar depression was. I didn't know what mom was going through emotionally. I'm sure she was processing her own feelings about her relationships and parenting skills and going through her own struggles coming from a home with no real parental guidance herself.

As a pre-teen and teenager, or even a college student, I didn't have the mental capacity to put myself in mom's shoes, to try to see things from her perspective. I certainly didn't have enough life experience yet to relate.

All I knew is that it felt like she didn't care. That she was choosing herself over her kids. That I didn't have a mom and I was all alone.

After mom's third divorce, she got worse and was prescribed more and more medications. She ended up in a mental hospital for a while and had shock therapy at one point.

I remember one year when we checked her into a group home for people who were mentally unstable. The sadness and despair I felt when we walked in were palpable.

All I kept thinking was, "How could this be where my mom belongs? How can this be my life?"

And I still remember how it smelled in there. Like dirty gym socks, body odor, and stale air.

The whole time we were there, I couldn't wait to leave. I felt so much shame and was resentful and disappointed and sad for the relationship I would never have with her.

She wasn't able to emotionally be there for me through my wedding, the birth of my children, my own divorce, or any other challenge I faced as an adult.

I deeply felt the loss of a mother to rely on and share my feelings with during those pivotal moments in my life... especially when I saw friends or other women who had a close, loving relationship with their mother.

Now, at 65, she's in an assisted living facility, her brain so scrambled that she basically just exists. I can't have a real, constructive conversation with her about this.

It's so incredibly ironic because I feel like the work I've done around my own internal emotional intelligence and mindset could finally help me better understand her.

I know she has a mental illness, and I do understand now that this contributed to her actions. But I also believe that there were conscious choices she made in her life that shaped who she was as a woman and a mother.

I will always believe that she could have made some of those choices differently.

She could have chosen to come home from work and spend time with us instead of going out.

She could have chosen not to bring strange men home when we were there.

She could have chosen to come home with the car when she had promised I could use it.

She could have made a thousand different choices and put us ahead of her selfish desires.

It's a horrible internal struggle for me. On the one hand, she's my mother and I care about her. But on the other hand, I feel zero connection to her. Zero.

I only visit a couple of times a year, mostly for birthdays or Christmas, and that's because I feel obligated to see her.

I feel so much regret for my boys, who will never have a "normal" grandmother. They have no relationship with her. She was never able to do things with them that would have built any sort of bond.

But I'm finally allowing myself to forgive. Not to excuse her behavior, but to forgive so I can move past this. To forgive so I can let go of the disappointment and regret over not having the childhood I thought every child deserves.

Now I am finding ways to learn from my life experiences, rather than letting them control me or define who I am.

I'm writing this book because experiences like this leave us with severe limiting beliefs that are always there, living in our subconscious. Many times, we aren't even aware of them.

And I know that so many women out there grew up with situations that are similar to mine. Who have struggled in the ways I have struggled and are trying to find their way.

If this book helps just one of them, it will be worth it to share my story, even if it might be hard for me to write and for some of my family to read.

Part of the work I've done over the last few years has been to uncover the limiting beliefs that this experience has given me so I can learn from them.

That's the starting point, to even know what they are so you can be aware when they are showing up.

The biggest and overarching limiting belief is that I am destined to turn out like her.

Every time I make a mistake, in life or with my kids, I hear that voice in my head that says, "You are just like her," or "You are going to turn out just like her." And it terrifies me. It makes me feel like I have to be perfect as a woman and a mother.

It's been an incredibly tough road, both surviving my childhood and finding the strength inside me to heal and grow from it.

I've made a lot of mistakes along the way.

I've had to fight my own addictive tendencies and lack of self-love that perpetuated destructive behaviors. I've had to deal with the consequences from some of them as well.

But I'm finally at a point where I've chosen to find the lessons in my experience with my mom. To see them as learning opportunities.

To ask "What is this teaching me?" instead of "Why is this happening to me?"

We can't go back and rewrite our beginning, but we can write a new ending. That's what this book is for me. The beginning of a new ending.

And in order to do that, in order to write a courageous new ending to my story, I had to first become aware of who I really was, and what my past had taught me. I had to break down those walls and allow all parts of me to co-exist.

It took a turning point moment shortly after my divorce for me to really be able to speak freely about this, and to show up as my most authentic self.

It was a sunny, winter day and I had just gotten to work. My boys were young then, maybe 10 and 6 years old. They had gotten off to school without fighting that morning and I remember feeling grateful for that.

I had just taken a new role at work, and the divorce had only been final for a short while, so I was still going through a lot emotionally. More responsibility in all areas of my life.

But that day, I was early to work, the sun was shining, and life was good.

Until I stepped out of the car.

There it was - one brown boot and one black boot.

Home was an hour away from the office and I had a meeting starting in 15 minutes. No time to go change my boots or even to go to the store and buy new shoes.

I struggled for a few minutes. My first reaction was complete embarrassment.

There I go, failing again! How could I be so stupid! Etc., etc.

But then I took a deep breath.

And I realized that I had no choice. I had to go into that office wearing two different boots. No matter what happened.

And you know what? No one even noticed!

The few that did had a story of their own of some clothing mishap they had. It actually built a stronger connection with them.

That day changed my life. Something so simple as mistakenly wearing two different boots flipped my entire perspective.

That's when I knew that I had crossed over.

I was no longer young and fearful of what other people think of me.
I was in control of my own destiny.
I could choose a different life.

When I reflect on my life, I see how this experience has made me who I am today.

And I believe that life's challenges shape us, and every choice we make leads us down the path we were meant to take in life.

I can't explain why my mom's path is the one that she ended up on; but I know that some of the choices she made led her there.

If I'm truly honest with myself, there's a part of me that doesn't regret going through this experience.

If I had had a simpler childhood, if I had a mother who was functional and available, I'd be someone totally different.

And I'm finally learning to love who I am today.

***

In this book, I'm going to share with you ten of the lessons I've learned from the years of living in my mother's shadow.

Each lesson has been a pivotal part of my journey to become the best version of me.

They have brought me awareness and understanding of how my experiences have shaped who I am.

From each of these lessons, I've formed personal mantras.

By definition, a personal mantra is *an affirmation to motivate and inspire you to be your best self.*

These personal mantras are ones I repeat on a regular basis to reinforce how far I've come and to strengthen my own self-awareness.

I'll end each chapter by sharing the mantras I've created from that particular lesson with you.

As you read this book, I encourage you to reflect on the lessons I share and how they might resonate with your own life experiences.

Use the mantras I share, or create your own that speak to your life experience.

Find a way to tell yourself every day how strong you are and how much you have overcome.

I hope my journey helps bring light to your darkness, as it did for me.

> *Our histories are never all good or all bad, and running from the past is the surest way to be defined by it. That's when it owns us. The key is bringing light to the darkness. Developing awareness and understanding.*
> *- Brene Brown*

~ 2 ~

LESSON 1: DO AS I SAY, NOT AS I DO

Living with a parent who is emotionally absent and in their own world makes it hard for us as children to understand our boundaries. We see them doing things that "good" parents should never do.

We are expected not to follow in their footsteps but to instead obey orders and do the things that we aren't seeing in action.

Growing up with my mom was truly a manifestation of the old saying, "Do As I Say, Not As I Do."

I really struggled with this with my mother, especially as a pre-teen and a teen. She was engaging in very risky behavior after her second divorce and it conflicted so much with what I thought a mother should be.

She'd go out drinking almost every night and bring home random guys to our apartment. It was a pretty run-down apartment and the bathroom was tiny, sandwiched between my bedroom and my mom's.

The bathroom had two doors on it, one leading to each room. The one that led to my room had a broken lock on it, so I would lay in my bed and hold the covers tight, listening to the sounds from mom's room and wishing the strange men would leave.

I distinctly remember the fear I felt, the feel of the blankets tucked up as far as I could under my chin. How hard it was to fall asleep. How I often cried and wished that I could just have a normal mom who would tuck me in and kiss me goodnight and go watch TV or read before she went to bed.

I would lay there in the dark, picturing my unicorn collection on my dresser, and the posters on the wall of Kirk Cameron and Bon Jovi. Finding comfort in the things I loved as a teenager.

And praying that no one would come into my room.

Once it actually happened. One of those men tried to come through that door, I heard the doorknob turn. I froze, in fear, terrified of what might happen next.

He never opened the door all the way. I don't know for sure why, but I'm grateful for that every time I reflect on that time period of my life.

The fact that my mother would do that when I was there in the apartment, made me feel alone and very much that she didn't care what happened to me.

I would often get angry. I would journal about it and how frustrated I was. I would feel so disgusted by what a bad example she was setting for us. I couldn't understand why she couldn't see that.

I sometimes wondered if she even really ever wanted to have kids.

I found my old journal just a few weeks ago and read some of it. The angst behind the words made me sad for that frightened little girl. And strengthened my resolve to find a way to always be there for my boys so they never have to feel alone like that.

The lesson I took away in my younger years from this is that I could choose to live and raise my own children differently. I wouldn't be a hypocrite as I so often thought she was.

I swore that my children would only see me as a positive role model, that they wouldn't be scared of the people I brought around them or worried about the choices I made.

Cue the limiting belief, "I have to be perfect to be a good mom."

When I became a mom myself, this limiting belief manifested in many ways.

I would beat myself up for every mistake I made, every misstep that happened when the boys were around.

It was all my fault, if only I had been a better mom, if only I had done this or that differently.

If only...

If I had a few drinks with family, I would worry about what my boys thought, what I was teaching them.

If I yelled at them out of frustration, I would immediately berate myself for losing my cool. I would be anxious and afraid that I was going to become just like my mom, and that I couldn't handle my children.

If I forgot something for school or missed paying a bill, I'd worry that they would see me as irresponsible, and that all of the other moms were judging me.

I was constantly second-guessing myself, asking too many questions, worrying too much about them when they make their own mistakes, and generally overthinking things.

I've come to learn that a lot of this is a part of parenting as a whole. But that took me putting myself out there and talking to people about where I felt I was failing. I had to humble myself and reach out to other moms in my network. To share stories of the parenting struggles I have.

Being aware of it and putting it out there was a huge help on my journey. I am finally more aware when these feelings start to creep in and am able to put them in perspective in a healthier way.

I'm still a work in progress here, but as I've been on my journey of self-exploration, I'm realizing what a fallacy that saying is, "Do As I Say, Not As I Do." It's an impossible standard to uphold.

In reality, we are imperfect by nature as human beings. Parenting is no exception. There is no rulebook. We are going to mess up.

Yes, I saw my mom make some really bad choices. And I made my own decisions and judgments about her behavior.

I saw my Dad make some really bad choices too. Alcohol was very prevalent in my life and it affected me and my behavior too, especially after my divorce.

I've made some bad choices of my own. Some that were visible to my boys, and some that were not.

My boys will make their own decisions and form their own judgments about what they saw from me.

But what I can do differently, what my mom never modeled for me, or even told me I should do, is to talk to my kids about my mistakes. To humble myself and let them see me as human.

And of course, to do my best to learn from my mistakes and not repeat the same ones over and over.

It took a while for me to talk openly about my struggles and let people inside my head. I credit some of that to the TED talk I stumbled on early in my self-evolution journey.

It was a 20-minute TED talk by Dr. Brene Brown. On the power of vulnerability. If you haven't watched it yet, Google it and watch it. I promise it will be worth your time.

I cried the whole way through it, thinking that she had just given me the greatest gift. The gift of realizing that I needed to bring all of the pieces of my life together. To live into who I was, the good, the bad and the ugly.

When we talk about the things that we feel shame about, we take away their power over us.

Admitting that we struggle and allowing ourselves to be vulnerable is the first step to claiming our power back.

My Mantras From Lesson 1:

I Will Not Do As My Mother Did, Or Even As She Said

I Will Do And Say In The Ways I Know Are Right For Me And For My Family

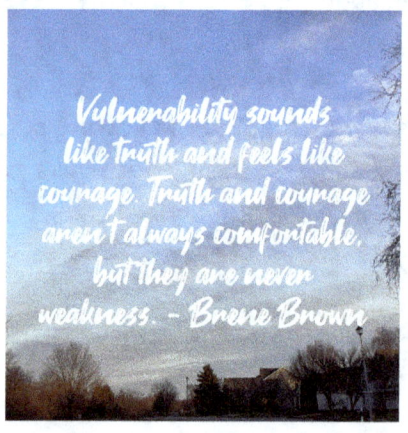

~ 3 ~

LESSON 2: MY PAST DOES NOT DEFINE ME

The experience I had with my mother does not define who I am.

I repeat that to myself often.

As I was building my own adult life, I lived in the shadow of mom's influence for many years. For the first few years, I didn't even realize it.

To be fair, It wasn't just my mother's influence, although hers had the strongest impact on me.

My father and his alcoholism also shaped me. The feeling of disappointment I would have when he'd call the morning he was supposed to pick us up for the weekend and cancel because he was "sick" is with me to this day. It's one of the reasons I find it so hard to rely on others.

My father died tragically, after years of not really taking care of himself or dealing with his own demons. I didn't know myself back then, the year he passed was several years before I started to figure life out. I have a lot of regret over not being in a healthy place emotionally to help him when he probably needed me most.

But I've come to realize that my childhood, and the events of my past with both my mother and my father, are only a piece of the puzzle for me.

These events do not define me. I am my own person, independent of those experiences.

They absolutely shaped my life and the lens through which I see things. But I have control over whether I let that influence affect how I react to the challenges that life throws at me.

This can be a tough lesson for most of us.

Many people don't know any other way. Their past may have been awful, uncomfortable, or even tragic, but it's what they know. Facing it head-on and dealing with it so they can push through is incredibly scary.

It's easier to just resign themselves to the fact that they can't change their circumstances.

I believe this is why some people cling to the belief that they are victims. That they are destined to follow the footsteps of their parents or family members.

Because these things happened to them growing up, they think they can't make themselves better. They have an excuse to not live their best life.

I refuse to do that. And you should too!

Your past does not define you. You are not your mother, father, aunt, uncle, grandmother, etc. You are not the events of your childhood. You are not even the mistakes you've made as an adult.

You have your own mind and power over your own choices. You have the ability to change your path.

Life is truly the sum of our choices. I write my blog about that. It's a reflection of the lessons that ordinary things in life teach us, and how we can choose to see things differently.

Choosing to believe that I am not defined by my past is probably the most important choice I have ever made.

Instead of asking myself "Why is this happening to me?" I choose to ask myself "What is this trying to teach me?"

I am choosing to learn from what my past taught me.

To apply those learnings to all areas of my own life, to use them to understand how I react to situations and why I parent the way I do.

I choose to become stronger because of my past, not a victim of it.

My Mantras From Lesson 2:

My Past Does Not Define Me

I Learn From Every Misstep And Mistake

~ 4 ~

LESSON 3: I AM NOT, NOR WILL I EVER BE, MY MOTHER

For all of you reading who had a mother who wasn't emotionally there for you, repeat after me:

I FORGE MY OWN PATH AND DO NOT FOLLOW IN HER FOOTSTEPS.

Say that as many times as you need to, every day for the rest of your life if you have to.

Put it on a post-it-note on your bathroom mirror, in your car, on your coffee pot, anywhere you will see it every day and hear it in your head.

Your brain is a muscle and repeating phrases that build us up are the exercises we need to do to maintain a positive, growth mindset.

I'll admit, this has been the most deeply rooted and difficult limiting belief for me to overcome. Its shadow was the darkest and largest for me through the years.

I spent many years of my life terrified that I would turn out just like my mother.

I built walls that hid all of the things from my past from others, only showing them the parts of me that I thought would make them proud.

It took years to break down those walls. But I realized as I got to know myself, that the walls had to come down for me to truly be who I am destined to be. Complete, yet imperfect. And beautiful.

Even now, at 45, with so many great things in my life - a successful career, my own home, and two smart, assertive, headstrong, teenage boys who have their whole lives ahead of them, I sometimes am still that scared little girl watching her mom fall apart and worrying that this is who I'm destined to become.

For years, I lived in her shadow. Afraid that I would become just like her.

Every time my kids messed up in school or made a bad choice, my first thought was that I've failed as a mother and I'm going to turn out just like her.

Every time I failed at a relationship, my first thought was that I've failed as a woman and I'm going to end up just like her. I was destined to be thrice-divorced, mentally unstable and alone.

Every time I failed at work, my first thought was that I'm not smart enough, I'm not strong enough emotionally, I'm a fraud, how could they put so much trust in me, I'm going to end up just like her.

That voice in my head was so loud, trying to tell me,

I'M JUST LIKE HER!

But I'm NOT!

It took a lot of practice and self-reflection, but now that I am aware of this limiting belief and can sense it when it's happening, that thought is fleeting. It doesn't bring me down in the same way it did just a few years ago.

I have learned to recognize when that anxious feeling starts to build up and to listen carefully, for that inner voice.

I have gained the confidence to pause and reflect on what it's trying to say and recognize the trigger for what it is.

This is the key to shutting it down. To expose that voice to the facts.

To acknowledge what is happening and to flip my perspective.

Whenever that voice tries to tell me that I'm going to be just like her, I stop and I say:

That's a lie, and you know it! There is no truth, no validity to this.

Look at all I've done that's been different!

- Look at how far I've come in my career
- Look at how great my boys are doing
- Look at my beautiful home
- Look at where I am at this point in my life vs. where she was
- Look at how much more I know about myself
- Look at how much healthier I am when dealing with my emotions

There is no truth to what that voice is saying. It is a lie trying to hold me back from being my best self.

Everyone who knows me and knows my story tells me the same thing. They often can't believe that I ever doubt myself.

I can hide it very well after so many years of practice. My walls are strong.

Ironically, there are a few ways that I am a bit like my mother, and I've come to realize that in these ways it's not a negative thing.

Part of the journey of self-awareness also requires us to find the things that are positive in all situations.

- My mother taught me to never go to bed without a hug and an "I love you."

- My mother was a beautiful young woman. I like to think that I got some of my own beauty from her.
- My mother was a very affectionate woman and wanted to love and be loved. I get that from her.
- My mother loved sweet tea. So do I.

And, my mother also taught me that my children deserve better than what she was able to give to me.

Sometimes when I think about those things, it's bittersweet. But it doesn't change the fact that there are so many things about her that I never want to be.

That's why this will probably always be the hardest limiting belief for me. I will likely never silence that voice completely.

But I can keep it pretty quiet and when it does try to talk, shut it down quickly now.

And that's made such a difference in my ability to have a positive mindset.

This lesson gives me two of my most powerful mantras.

My Mantras From Lesson 3:

I Am Not, Nor Will I Ever Be, My Mother

I Can Choose How Much I Let Her Influence Me

~ 5 ~

LESSON 4: JUST BECAUSE SHE GAVE BIRTH TO ME, I'M NOT OBLIGATED TO SPEND TIME WITH HER

Those of you reading this, who grew up with similar situations, have probably heard many people tell you "she's your mother, you have to spend time with her!"

I believe that's a horrible thing for people to say, even for those who love you. They don't know what you've been through or how you are feeling, or how her actions have affected you.

It's not fair for any of them to pass judgment on you or try to shame you into doing something that you don't want to do.

I spent many years wrestling with the battle between obligation and guilt and my own sanity.

I've built my own life now, and the people in it need my head in a good space.

I am sorry if some of you may feel that it is heartless that I don't spend a lot of time with my mom.

I am sorry that you can't understand why I don't want to see her.

What you don't realize is that it hurts every time I'm in the same room with her.

And I refuse to be sorry for putting my own family first, for putting my self-care and mental health ahead of some false feeling of obligation.

Finally, at 45 years old, I'm prioritizing what's more important in my life.

She cannot take that away from me. I no longer give her that power.

She is in a place where she is taken care of, she has made many of her own choices in life that brought her to where she is today.

It's sometimes hard for me when my brother, who still visits her often and goes out of his way to do things for her, asks me to go visit her.

It's even harder for me to explain to him why I don't want to see her. It's hard for me to explain the shame and anger and resentment I still feel.

Which often results in me agreeing to do it. Then suffering through a visit with her, and crying all the way home, all of the old memories and pain flooding back.

I know it's hard for him too, though, and I try to see things from his perspective. We all grew up with her, and even though we had different experiences in the way we processed what was happening, she still influenced all of us.

Holidays are the worst.

Especially Mother's Day.

It's a double-edged sword for me. It not only brings up all the feelings I have about my mom, but it also triggers the insecurities I have about my own parenting.

I stand in the greeting card aisle and I try not to let the tears fall.

Card after card that gushes about mothers. Sappy cards that go on and on about how much mom did for us, what a wonderful influence she has been on our lives, what a perfect grandmother she is. And how much we want to be like her when we have kids of our own.

It's like a dagger straight to my heart.

The guilt and resentment that I feel for not having those sweet sentiments about my mom can be overwhelming sometimes.

I try to find the most generic Mother's Day card I can and hightail it out of there as quickly as possible.

I wonder what the people around me think, or if they can read the emotions on my face or in my body language. Some probably can. Some may even be going through the same things as I do, in the very same aisle.

And then I overthink Mother's Day at home. Expecting my boys (who are teenagers) to make some grandiose gesture for me. And when they don't, I feel let down and guilty all over again.

Sometimes I wish we could just skip Mother's Day altogether.

I have been through therapy to talk about this. I have written it all out, journaled about it, reflected on it, and I fully understand why I feel this way. I've got a healthy perspective now, but it doesn't change the fact that I still feel it.

I love her because she is the woman who gave birth to me.

I care about her because she is a human being.

Without her, I would not exist. Nor would my children, or the life I have built for them.

But the blood tie does not mean I have to ignore the fact that being with her doesn't feel emotionally safe for me. It doesn't bring me joy, it only makes my heart hurt.

I have to love myself and my children enough to set boundaries. To be courageous enough to put myself and my emotional wellness first in this situation.

To all of you reading this who are struggling with the same issue, I encourage you to do the same.

It's okay to prioritize yourself over the people in your life who are damaging to you.

They do not deserve to have that much power over you.

That realization has been a powerful one for me. I'm so much stronger now in all situations in life since I have accepted this. It's easier for me to say no to the things I don't want to do, and to practice self-care when I need it.

To be my best self, I know that I can't give up my life to take care of her, or go out of my way to see her when my heart isn't in it.

And that's okay. I've come to terms with that. Even if other people haven't.

My Mantras From Lesson 4:

I Will Be There For My Boys So They Want to Always Be There For Me

I Will Never Force Them to Do Anything That Makes Their Heart Hurt

~ 6 ~

LESSON 5: THIS TOTALLY SUCKS FOR MY KIDS

This is another area where I feel like my kids got the short end of the stick.

And another area that has made me feel guilty so many times in the past.

My boys will never have a "normal" grandmother on my side of the family.

You know, the traditional kind that bakes you cookies and takes you fun places and lets you stay up too late. Snuggles you with a blanket and all the hugs and kisses you can handle.

I didn't either, to be honest. My grandmother had her hands full with her own children and their issues.

Once I was old enough to have children, my mom was basically incapable of taking care of her herself, let alone able to form a relationship with my children.

She no longer had a driver's license or a comfortable home where the boys could go. She was very overweight and not able to run and play with them.

I would try to take the boys to see her, but she just wanted them to sit in her lap and snuggle with her. They were young, spirited boys and they couldn't sit still that long.

She couldn't understand that and would continually make me feel guilty because my boys didn't want to just sit with her.

I couldn't let them stay overnight with her and she couldn't take them on adventures.

They never had a relationship with her growing up, and that made me sad.

I'm grateful that my boys have both of their grandparents on their dad's side of the family. A generous, loving set of grandparents who do lots of things for them and with them.

That helps a little.

But I still have a lot of regret for the traditional extended family that my boys don't really have. My father died much too young when the boys were only 6 and 2, and he barely got to know them.

So they didn't have a grandfather on my side of the family to spend time with either.

It all makes me sad if I think too hard about it.

Over the years, I've come to terms with it, though, and the more people I spend time with, the more I realize that a "traditional" family is just an illusion.

My boys have other adults in our families that they can spend time with, look up to, and shape their lives in positive ways.

Unfortunately, I held onto that sadness and regret for a really long time in my life. I finally feel like it's working its way out of my system.

I'm learning how important it is to let go of the disappointment we feel that our lives don't match up to whatever fantasy world we dreamt up that was the opposite of what we had.

There's not really a true "normal" family. Every single family has its issues, some just hide them better than others.

The grandmothers we see on old TV shows really don't exist. Maybe they never did.

For sure mine will never be one. And my boys will grow up without that.

But they have me and I love them fiercely. I will do everything in my power to give them the best life possible, despite missing out on having the grandmother they deserve.

And I vow to be the best grandmother I can be for their kids someday.

My Mantras From Lesson 5:

This Mom Gig Doesn't Come With Instructions

I Will No Longer Let The Vision Of How I Think Life Should Have Been Have Power Over Me

~ 7 ~

LESSON 6: BEING A MOM IS HARD WORK AND THERE'S NO RULE BOOK

There is no right way to parent our children. There is no manual with step-by-step instructions on what to do when they mess up, or when we mess up.

Which happens plenty often.

Not having my mom around to guide me left me feeling very insecure about my own capabilities as a mother.

When my boys were babies, I felt like I had it under control. Feed them, clothe them, change their diapers, hug them, snuggle them, make sure they are comfortable when they sleep. Listen to them cry. Then listen to them cry some more.

It's simpler for the first few months to a year, until they start walking and exerting their independence.

Looking back now, I realize that my mom probably felt the same way. She was attentive and loving when we were little and didn't have minds of our own.

But when push came to shove and we started to become little human beings with thoughts and wants and needs and ideas, she floundered.

She wasn't mentally strong enough to deal with the challenges in life and guide us along the way.

I realize now that being a mom is really hard work.

It's hands-down the hardest job I've ever had, even harder than running an entire department and managing a 3 million dollar budget. That was a cakewalk compared to parenting.

I have two strong-willed, assertive, smart boys that I'm raising. And they sure know how to push buttons. Because they are trying to figure themselves out too.

I often overcompensate because I'm trying so hard to guide them.

When they were in elementary school, I was heavily involved in the PTO, participating in nearly every event, even though I was juggling a full-time job and a not-so-healthy marriage. I chaired committees, sat on the board, and loved every minute of it.

I attended every parent-teacher conference and tried to respond immediately to every email from their teachers when things went wrong in the classroom.

I wanted to be there for my kids in every way I could. So they never felt like they were alone. So they could be proud to have a mom who was always there for them.

Despite all of my efforts, and even now that they are teenagers, I still don't ever feel like I'm getting it quite right. There are so many different ways to handle each situation, like a choose your own adventure book. I used to love those when I was a kid!

Teenagers are hard!

It's sometimes difficult for me to let them fail and learn some of life's hard lessons on their own. Even though I know that's what's best for them.

I think somewhere inside me I feel like I need to always help them because I didn't have someone to help me.

What's ironic is that the freedom I had because of my own lack of guidance growing up taught me how to be independent, strong and resilient. And I want that for both of my boys too.

I sometimes wonder...

If there was a rulebook for Mom to follow, would things have been different?

Would I have been different?

Mom never had a guide in her life, either. I see that now. It took me years of reflection and self-development for me to be able to understand that.

There will be people who try to tell us how to parent. Who believe they know what's right.

Their intentions may be good but they don't live our lives. They aren't in our heads and they can't possibly know what's right for us.

We have to make our own rules. And we have to be confident in the fact that they are the right ones. If they don't work, we can change them.

That's the beautiful part of life.

Parenting is hard. It will always be hard.

All of my mom friends tell me that too. Regardless of how great of a childhood someone had, we're never really prepared for parenting. We're all just feeling our way through it.

But showing up as who we are and engaging with the world in a truly authentic way also teaches our children some serious life lessons. Ones that they don't learn in school.

The hardest part in my opinion is the waiting. The lessons that we try to teach them now may take awhile to percolate, to sink in, to actually appear in ways they can apply in their own lives.

I can only hope that my boys learn as much from their childhood about themselves as I did. And in much more positive ways!

Remember, we were given this life because we are strong enough to live it, and we are strong enough to parent them through it.

My Mantras From Lesson 6:

The Rules Of My Home Are What Work For Me And My Family

I Make My Own Rulebook

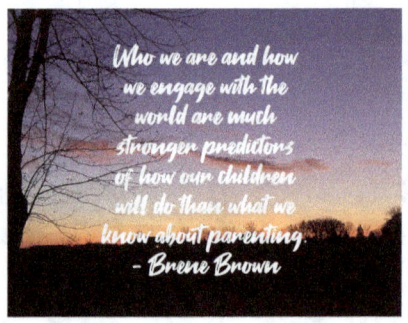

~ 8 ~

LESSON 7: I HAVE TO FIND MY OWN CLOSURE

Just like there are no rules for parenting, there are no rules for finding closure in situations like mine.

My mom is now in a place mentally where she can't have the conversation with me that I'm finally ready to have with her.

Yet I need closure.

Closure to be able to find peace and to forgive.
Closure to let go of the hurt and move on.

I realized that it won't just happen magically though. I have to find it for myself. I have to let go of the disappointment of not being able to hear an explanation or apology from her directly.

There are a few ways I'm working through this. Maybe some of you can take these and apply them in your own lives too.

I'm turning to resources that help me.

One of them is *The Grief Recovery Handbook*, by John W. James and Russell Friedman. I was introduced to this book by a dear friend who does grief recovery therapy.

It taught me that grieving doesn't always have to be about death. Traumatic incidents in our life are also grieving events and we need to process them in a very similar way.

I needed to grieve the childhood I never had.

I started by writing down the things that hurt me about my mom. And my Dad.

I made a list of the turning point moments in my life that affected me the most.

And I wrote her a letter.

One that I will never give to her, but one that provides me the catharsis that I need.

My niece and I have gone through similar life experiences, both having moms who weren't there for us the way we needed them. She's 18 years younger than me but has lived so much life and so much pain.

She wrote her own letter and we came together to read ours to each other this year.

And we cried.

- We cried for the relationship we would never have with our moms.
- We cried for the relationship our kids would never have with their grandmothers.
- We cried for the loss of our childhood so early in our lives.
- We cried for the fear and guilt and self-doubt this type of childhood instilled in us.

But we also grew stronger and more self-aware.

We knew that our experiences have shaped us into the women we are today. We knew that overcoming these challenges was one of the reasons why we are who we are today.

And we knew that just being in it together was a life-changing experience.

We read our letters, and then threw them into my fireplace and watched them burn, taking some of the pain with them.

That night, we found some of the closure we needed.

It gave our life experience perspective and boundaries.

Dealing with those emotions took away some of the control they had over us. And most importantly, it helped us to learn from them and be aware when our experiences were affecting our behavior with our own children and partners so we could course correct.

And those are all good outcomes.

It was a life-changing night when we read those letters to each other.

We had to take the steps to create that closure though, it didn't magically happen. It was hard and it was emotional.

But it was also necessary.

And it was powerful.

My Mantras From Lesson 7:

I Can Make My Own Closure, I Don't Need Her To Participate

I Can Learn To Forgive So I Can Move On

~ 9 ~

LESSON 8: IT'S OKAY FOR ME TO FORGIVE

For a long time, I thought I would never be able to forgive my mom for the way her behavior affected me.

She had hurt me so badly, and so negatively impacted my life and how I felt about myself. It all felt so very unfair.

But on my journey to become my best self, I kept seeing signs, articles, and social media posts about forgiveness, and how it's such an important part of the process.

I have a regular daily practice to build a positive mindset and a foundation of gratitude for my life.

I begin every day with a positive thought, and I share that out on my social media platforms to inspire both myself and others. And then I end every day with gratitude, reflecting on what was good about my day before I fall asleep.

This has been a game-changer in my life, helping me to stay grounded and focused and be able to have a foundation of peace in my life.

Through this practice, I have come to understand the importance of choosing my battles, of processing my feelings, and of not allowing toxic behavior or people to have power over me.

Through one of the connections I had formed with a woman I met in a coaching group, I came across this quote, "Forgiveness is letting go of the hope of a better yesterday." (credit: *The Grief Recovery Handbook*, John W. James and Russell Friedman).

It stopped me in my tracks when I first read it in the book.

Literally took my breath away with the truth in it.

Let me repeat that.

Forgiveness is letting go of the HOPE of a better yesterday

We can't go back. We can't change what happened in our past.

We will never have that childhood that we wished for so badly back then. We will never have that mother-daughter relationship that we so desperately needed.

There is only moving forward. There is only letting go.

And we need to do it for us, not for our mothers. Not for their peace of mind or to absolve them of their behavior.

But for our sanity and our ability to live our best possible lives.

The important thing to remember is that if you forgive, you aren't admitting your own failure. In fact, you are showing your strength.

You are proving to the world that this life experience doesn't define you.

You are letting go and moving forward. As your own, unique self. On your own two feet.

Forgiveness is probably one of the most challenging things we can do in life. But also the most necessary.

I've realized that I need to forgive both of my parents.

My dad for his alcoholism and how it cut his life so short.

He didn't live long enough to know his grandchildren and see them become the young men they are now. He didn't live long enough to be there for me either and for us to develop the relationship I wish I could have had with him.

With my Dad, it just makes me sad.

I don't harbor the same resentment and anger toward him. Maybe because he didn't live with us and I didn't see his behaviors every day. Or maybe it was because I could better empathize with him, as he grew up without a mother too.

It's easier for me to forgive him.

With Mom, it's a different story. Maybe it's because I'm a woman and a mother myself. The relationship is just different.

I wish I could read my mom the letter I wrote her. I wish with all my heart that she was mentally able to grasp it and to help me understand life from her perspective.

But that will never happen. It's too late now.

I'm learning to forgive her for that too. And to let go of the disappointment I feel for not being able to learn from her in that way.

But most importantly, more important than forgiving my mother or even my father, I am learning to forgive myself.

I'm forgiving myself, in the truest, most authentic sense of the word, for all of the mistakes I've made growing up, in my relationships, and in my parenting.
I'm forgiving myself for not giving myself the love and grace I needed along the way.
I'm forgiving myself for not taking care of that frightened little girl inside of me the way I should have.

And I'm finally learning to love who I am, flaws and all.

My Mantras From Lesson 8:

I Forgive So I Can Let Go Of The Disappointment And Regret

I Forgive For My Own Peace Of Mind, Not to Excuse Her

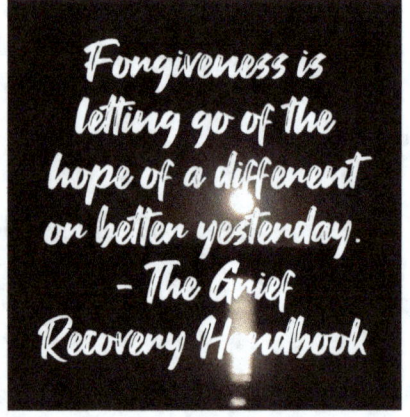

~ 10 ~

LESSON 9: LIFE MUST GO ON...I CHOOSE TO LEARN FROM IT

The thing about experiences like this is that they can affect our lives in one of two ways.

We can become victims of our circumstances. Or we can rise above them.

Growing up, there were so many people in my extended family that chose to become victims.

I'd watch them play the pity card, to have every excuse to not make good choices. And they would continue to perpetuate bad behaviors, seemingly indifferent to the effect it had on their lives and the lives of those around them.

It disgusted me honestly. I couldn't understand why they would choose to live that way.

It didn't seem that hard to me to make different choices.

To choose to learn from your environment and experience and make a life for yourself.

It doesn't take money to do that. You just have to choose to do things differently.

Even now, after so many years of adulthood, of living and learning and striving to make more of myself, I struggle to relate to people who play the victim.

I can do a better job now of trying to understand their underlying motivation, and recognizing the influences they had that might have affected them.

But that doesn't change the fact that we ultimately do have control of so much in our lives. We define our paths by the choices we make.

My path has been bumpy, and winding and I've gotten lost a few times along the way.

But, I'm finally coming to the point though where I think I can let go of my past and truly move on.

I choose to learn from these experiences and let them influence my life in a positive way.

To let them guide me to ask, "What is this trying to teach me?" not "Why is this happening to me?"

To be able to pause when things trigger me, understand where they are coming from, and consciously choose how to react.

I choose to learn from all of it. I choose me and my boys and my happiness over dwelling on the shame of my past.

All of the other mothers out there who are reading this book, not knowing whether you can bring yourself up and out of that life experience...know that you can.

Every day is a new opportunity to think differently. To make different choices, to take small steps to get yourself out of your current situation.

Every situation is a learning experience and an opportunity to grow stronger.

You are not alone in this journey. There are many of us out there.

Join me in my Facebook Group (Two Different Boots), seek out moms in your neighborhood (you'd be surprised who you already know who's been through this!), call your best friend. Find those members of your family who have risen above if they are out there.

Just reach out and talk about it. Show up and be vulnerable. That's what will make you strong.

Choose to move on and learn from your life. Don't become a victim.

My Mantras From Lesson 9:

I Choose To Learn From My Experiences and Not Let Them Define Me

I Choose To Make Choices That Make My Life Better

~ 11 ~

LESSON 10: I AM NOT ALONE

One of the other limiting beliefs I took away from my childhood was this:

It won't get done right if I don't do it myself. I can't rely on anyone else.

I was let down so often during my childhood that I began to feel like I couldn't rely on anyone.

Lots of times it was my Dad when he said he would come to pick us up for the weekend and then called to cancel.

But it was also my Mom, when she was out running around instead of home with me, or when she left without telling me where she was going and didn't bring the car home so I could go to the concert. Or when she was too messed up in the head, engulfed in her own problems to be there for me the way a mother should be there for her daughter.

I didn't have anyone to fall back on to help me. Or at least that's the way I felt growing up.

To my family reading this, I know some of you will disagree. You'll say I could have just called or come over or asked for help at any time.

But as a child, a teenager, and a young adult, I didn't know how. I felt like asking for help would bring shame on my family and on me. All I knew is that I was going to have to learn to be strong enough to do it all myself.

I'm not even sure I would have known what to ask for back then either.

How does a pre-teen/teenage girl ask for the guidance she doesn't even know she needs? All I knew is that I felt an emptiness, a loneliness, an ache inside, like something was missing.

Somewhere deep inside I think I also felt that I didn't deserve it. That I wasn't good enough for people to help me. After all, I was just a poor girl from a poor family (isn't that a quote from a Queen song?).

I carried that with me into adulthood. Into my marriage and my experience as a mother. Into how I parented my children. I looked for that guidance and recognition in all the wrong places.

I know I'm not alone in that experience either. So many women who grew up without guidance seek attention in destructive ways.

Alcohol was my vice for many years. After my divorce, I spent many weekends when the boys were with their dad at parties or out singing karaoke. Alcohol helped me let go of the stress of my life and have more fun, be more outgoing, meet new people. It helped me forget all of my responsibilities and made me feel pretty and special.

Temporarily.

But none of it really filled the hole in my heart.

It's only beginning to close now because I'm finally learning to see (and love) the real me.

Therapy has helped a lot. Getting to know myself and what motivates me has helped even more.

After all of these years, I am finally realizing that I am not alone on this journey. Far from it.

There are literally millions of other women out there who have experienced similar childhoods, similar feelings, and similar limiting beliefs.

I've met a few of them in person, many more of them virtually. I've coached several of them.

Their stories are ones of tragedy, despair, and loneliness. But also stories of courage, hope, and strength.

So many of them, like me, chose to learn from their journeys. To rise above their circumstances and raise their children differently. To find themselves in the midst of all of the chaos and make it to the other side with strength and dignity.

For those of you I haven't met or talked to: If you haven't found yourself yet - **Don't give up.**

There's still time. Every day is a new day and an opportunity to make a different choice.

The first step is knowing that you can.

My journey may sound like yours, with some variations. It may sound like millions of others too.

I take comfort in the fact that others can relate and empathize with my pain and my self-discovery.

And I hope that sharing my story will give that same comfort to other women who need it.

All of us who have been on this journey and came out stronger on the other side should be proud.

I know I'm proud of who I've become and I'm proud to be able to share this story.

> *But most of all, I'm proud to be finally stepping out of my mother's shadow and learning to love the woman I see.*

~ 12 ~

LIFE BEYOND THE LESSONS

Throughout this book, I've shared with you the key lessons I took away from my life experience with my mom and how it shaped my life.

While each individual lesson taught me something different, I also wanted to talk about the collective influence all of our life experiences (and the lessons they teach us) can have on who we become.

Living through all of the trauma, the pain, the frustration, the resentment, the guilt, and the tears, made me who I am.

I like to think I've taken the best of what I gained from my parents and that those pieces, along with the self-discovery I have done, make me a better person.

And for that I am grateful.

A few years ago, I made a physical list of the things I love about myself. I add to it occasionally as life evolves.

I keep both an email folder and a paper file folder of compliments and successes I have had in my life.

Now when that voice in my head tries to tell me that I'm going to end up becoming like my mother, manifesting all of the things that I so desperately want to NOT be, I pull these out and look at them.

Reading the notes from my coworkers, my friends, my group members, seeing pictures of me and my boys doing things that make us smile, all helps me stay focused and positive.

Having this tangible documentation of the good things in my life serves as a reminder that people who go through hard things can learn from them and come out stronger.

Because of my experiences, I am strong and capable of dealing with life's challenges.

Because of my experiences, I am a better mother.
Because of my experiences, I am a better friend.
Because of my experiences, I am a better partner.
Because of my experiences, I am a better leader, teacher, and coach.

Make yourself a list that reminds you of all of the strength you've gained from your struggles.

It can be a game-changer when you need it.

As human beings, we are meant to struggle. I firmly believe that.

We may not understand why when it's happening to us. We may feel like it's all too much.

But without our struggles, we wouldn't truly recognize or appreciate the beauty in the simple, wonderful moments of life.

Our struggles are what make us strong.

YOU are strong!

~ 13 ~

CONCLUSION

I wrote this book not because I wanted people to feel sorry for me, pity me, or offer me sympathy.

I wrote this book as an example for women everywhere that it is possible to overcome the circumstances from our childhoods that threaten to devour us, to bury us, to hide who we are meant to be.

I wrote this book to encourage and lift up those of you who need a voice in your head that tells you it's all going to be okay. That you are strong enough.

I hope you read it all the way through and take pieces away that can help you in your own life.

And then I hope you read it again and find more pieces that help you as you grow.

Some of the things I've done to break these patterns are so very simple. Yet they can be really hard to implement.

It takes courage and a strong mindset.

But the good news is that our brain is a muscle. It can be trained and rewired and taught to think differently.

Changing the way we think just a little bit every day can make all the difference.

May this book be your starting point. The first step in your journey.

And a guidebook for you along the way if you need one.

* * *

I'm here if you need me - even if you just want to share your story.

You can reach out to me in lots of different ways - pick your favorite.

I'd love to hear from you!

- Facebook Business Page: www.facebook.com/twodifferentboots
- Facebook Group: www.facebook.com/groups/twodifferentboots
- LinkedIn: www.linkedin.com/in/1michellesmith
- Blog: www.sumofourchoices.com
- Email: twodifferentboots@gmail.com

~ 14 ~

EPILOGUE

Just 35 days after publishing this book, on February 4, 2021, my mother passed away, at only 65-years-old.

She died peacefully in her sleep, her heart and body finally having been through enough. She had been under hospice care for the better part of a year and her health was progressively deteriorating.

I've been going through pictures and what little she had in the tiny room she was in at the assisted living facility. Finding fragments of moments from my childhood, some that I had forgotten and others that are so vivid they could have happened yesterday.

Mom lived a hard life. She was surrounded by severe dysfunction herself growing up. She didn't get the nurturing and support she needed either as a child.

And she made a lot of choices that were not in the best interest of her children.

My brothers and I deserved better. Even if some of her issues were outside of her control.

But over the past year, I've been able to reflect on her life and the life experiences I've now lived through and try to put myself in her shoes in a different way.

I understand now how hard it is to be a woman and a mother. And to do it with a mental illness and very little support must have felt impossible to her sometimes.

Two days before she passed, I went to see her for the last time.

I sat there with her and held her hand and thought about all of the self-development I've done over the past few years. How much more I know now about myself and who I am.

And I tried to put myself in her shoes. Her at my age and younger, trying to navigate motherhood, suffering from a mental illness and virtually no support around her.

I held her hand and I told her I was sorry that she struggled so hard. That I was grateful to her for giving birth to me and that if she had been a different mother, I wouldn't be who I am today.

Which is true.

And I'm finally learning to love the woman I have become.

I was finally able to let go of the anger and the hurt. To forgive, not to excuse her or to forget how this experience shaped me, but to let go of the disappointment I feel for not having the childhood I deserved.

I am so grateful I was able to have those last few moments with her to say goodbye and, even though she was non-responsive that day, I hope she heard me.

And I hope maybe she found a little peace in those words too.

It's an interesting kind of grief in a situation like this.

The emotions come in waves and are a mixture of relief and a deep sense of sadness and loss for a childhood (and adulthood for her) that should have been much different.

I take a deep breath when the waves come over me.

And then I take another..and another...as many as it takes and for as long as it takes to process this and adjust to life in this next chapter.

* * *

If you are going through (or have gone through) an experience with a parent like this, I hope you have found encouragement in my story.

I hope you have learned that it's okay to feel all of those emotions we feel, to be hurt and sad and scared.

And I also hope you know that it is possible, and necessary, to rise above those emotions, to find the learnings and to push yourself to take your power back.

Because you deserve to have a happy, productive life. And so do your children…and their children.

Break the pattern.

I believe in you.

~ 15 ~

ACKNOWLEDGMENTS

Even though my childhood was hard and there were many painful moments, there were still many people in my life who inspired me and helped me on my journey.

I'd like to thank a few of them here.

To my son, Ryder, for designing the cover of this book. Your creative eye saw exactly what I wanted to express.

And to both of my boys - my sweet, smart, stubborn, independent young men. For putting up with me your entire lives. For dealing with my endless questions and the way I tend to overthink things. For sharing your childhoods with me and for (hopefully) learning more than I did and walking away with a balanced perspective on life.

To my stepfather, Mark, thank you for being a guiding influence on my academic career. For pushing me to be the smartest, most successful woman I could be. And for always being proud of me, even when I wasn't strong enough to carry the proverbial milk jug.

To my aunt, Jo, who was the mother I never had in my adult years. Even though it wasn't the same, and didn't fill that hole I felt, you gave me the support I so badly needed in some very important areas of my life. And you still give me the advice and the ear I need to listen when I struggle even now.

To my brothers, Chris and Mark Jr, for being there with me along the way. For suffering in your own ways and taking your own learnings from this journey. I thank you for always being there for me, and couldn't imagine my life without you.

To my best friend, Randalyn, for living life by my side in junior high, and for sticking with me all of these years after. You saw inside my life in a way very few people did, and you still wanted to be my friend. You were a shoulder for me to cry on, then and now. And you never judge me as I struggle to be the best mom I can be and stumble more than a few times along the way.

To my niece, Samantha, who's gone through her own challenges with her emotionally absent mother, for being my partner in crime on this journey the last few years. For being vulnerable to dig deep with me and work through the sh*t we've had to work through. And for being the first person to read this book when I started writing it.

To my dear friend, Carrie, for all of the walks and talks on our journey together at the office. For commiserating with me about work, about my mom, about my dating life. We've shared so much as moms of boys and cohorts at work. I am forever grateful for tacos and Starbucks with you.

There are so many other wonderful people who have influenced my life as I've grown and learned and moved on. Too many to thank individually, but I hope I've expressed my gratitude personally in other ways so you know who you all are.

I love you all more than I could ever say.

~ 16 ~

ABOUT THE AUTHOR

Michelle is a single mom who lives in Oconomowoc, Wisconsin with her two boys, Ryder and Jacob.

This book is a life story, a sharing of the lessons she learned from her experiences with her mother, and hopefully a resource for other women who grew up without moms to find inspiration and encouragement.

Michelle is a leader at the office, sharing positivity and encouragement and bringing courageous authenticity to her work.

She writes a weekly blog that illustrates how ordinary moments in life can teach us lessons and help us view the world in a more positive way.

Michelle also manages a Facebook group where you can go for daily doses of positivity and true authentic communication.

And she runs her own freelance coaching business, Two Different Boots, where she facilitates group workshops and shares content that helps women find ways to grow a positive mindset, communicate authentically and become their best selves.

Michelle is a work in progress and continues to learn about herself every single day.

www.ingramcontent.com/pod-product-compliance
Lightning Source LLC
Chambersburg PA
CBHW072206100526
44589CB00015B/2395